I Can Wash My Face

Written by Chemise Taylor

Illustrated by Alexis B. Taylor

Copyright © 2019 by Autism Learners, LLC

Published by Autism Learners, LLC

All rights reserved. No part of this publication may be reproduced, distributed, or transmitted in any form or by any means, including photocopying, recording, or other electronic or mechanical methods, without the prior written permission of the publisher, except in the case of brief quotations embodied in critical reviews and certain other noncommercial uses permitted by copyright law.

First Printing, 2019.

ISBN: 978-1-951573-04-1

www.autismlearners.com

It's time for me to wash my face.

I go to the sink and turn on the faucet.

I wet my hands with water.

I get SOAP.

I lather the soap in my hands.

I rub the soap on my face.

I wash my face for....

20 to 30 seconds

I gather more water in my hands.

I rinse the soap off my face with the water.

I turn the faucet off.

I get a *towel.*

I dry my face.

Last but not least, I put lotion on my face.

All done! Now I'm ready for the day!

Book Details

Story Word Count: 98

Key Words: Wash, Face, Soap, Water, Hands, Towel, Dry, Lather

Comprehension Check
- What was the story about?
- What did he clean his face with?
- What did he dry his face with?

Reading Award

This certificate goes to:

_____

for reading "I Can Wash My Face"

Good Job!

Printable & Digital Worksheets | Flashcards | Books | Apps | More

www.autismlearners.com

www.ingramcontent.com/pod-product-compliance
Lightning Source LLC
Chambersburg PA
CBHW042110090526

44592CB00004B/79